MW00359033

ALL ABOUT SHARKS

PREHISTORIC SHARKS

by Yvette LaPierre

BrightPoint Press

San Diego, CA

BrightPoint Press

© 2023 BrightPoint Press
an imprint of ReferencePoint Press, Inc.
Printed in the United States

For more information, contact:
BrightPoint Press
PO Box 27779
San Diego, CA 92198
www.BrightPointPress.com

ALL RIGHTS RESERVED.

No part of this work covered by the copyright hereon may be reproduced or used in any form or by any means—graphic, electronic, or mechanical, including photocopying, recording, taping, web distribution, or information storage retrieval systems—without the written permission of the publisher.

LIBRARY OF CONGRESS CATALOGING-IN-PUBLICATION DATA

Names: LaPierre, Yvette, 1963- author.
Title: Prehistoric sharks / by Yvette LaPierre.
Description: San Diego, CA: BrightPoint Press, [2023] | Series: All about
   sharks | Includes bibliographical references and index. | Audience:
   Grades 10-12
Identifiers: LCCN 2022016074 (print) | LCCN 2022016075 (eBook) | ISBN
   9781678203665 (hardcover) | ISBN 9781678203672 (pdf)
Subjects: LCSH: Sharks--Juvenile literature. | Sharks--Juvenile literature.
   | Sharks--Evolution--Juvenile literature.
Classification: LCC QL638.9 .L365 2023 (print) | LCC QL638.9 (eBook) |
   DDC 597.3--dc23/eng/20220413
LC record available at https://lccn.loc.gov/2022016074
LC eBook record available at https://lccn.loc.gov/2022016075

CONTENTS

AT A GLANCE

- Sharks have lived on our planet for more than 400 million years.

- Paleontologists are scientists who study ancient life forms. They have found fossils of more than 2,000 species of prehistoric sharks. Those are sharks that lived before written human history.

- Teeth are the most common fossils of prehistoric sharks.

- Sharks have survived at least five mass extinction events.

- Many strange prehistoric sharks lived during the golden age of sharks 360 to 299 million years ago.

- The first modern-looking shark, *Cladoselache*, lived more than 350 million years ago.

- The prehistoric shark megalodon was the largest ocean predator that has ever lived.

- All sharks living today descended from prehistoric sharks.

- Some modern shark species have changed very little from their prehistoric relatives.

INTRODUCTION

ATTACK!

Ten million years ago (**MYA**), a huge shark patrolled warm tropical waters. Megalodon was hungry and looking for food. The shark spied a whale. The whale was big and powerful. But megalodon was even bigger and fiercer. At 60 feet (18 m) long, it was the largest hunter in the ocean.

Megalodon swung its massive tail fin and launched toward the whale. The shark opened its huge mouth. Hundreds of giant teeth in five rows lined its jaws. Megalodon bit down on the whale's jaw with tremendous force. It bit all the way through.

An illustration of megalodon hunting a whale

Megalodon was much larger than a modern great white shark.

Then its rows of sharp teeth gouged the whale's side, tearing off huge chunks of flesh. No creature, no matter how big, was safe from this monster of the sea.

ABOUT PREHISTORIC SHARKS

Sharks have swum Earth's oceans for more than 400 million years. They were around long before the dinosaurs. Sharks have been on Earth even longer than trees. Prehistoric means before written history.

The first prehistoric sharks **evolved** from the earliest fish. The fossil record shows many odd-looking sharks over nearly half a billion years of evolution. The earliest sharks looked more like eels. One ancient shark had a toothbrush-like fin on top of its head. Others had jaws like buzz saws or jagged craft scissors. One of the most famous prehistoric sharks is megalodon. It was three times larger than a great white shark. It had teeth as big as an adult's hands. The shark's tail fin was taller than a fully grown human. Megalodon was even bigger than a *Tyrannosaurus rex*. It was the largest ocean **predator** that has ever lived.

All sharks living today descended from prehistoric sharks. Scientists study shark fossils to learn more about these ancient sharks. These fossils give people an idea of what sharks may have looked like 400 MYA.

One megalodon tooth could be up to 7 inches (18 cm) long.

1

THE FIRST SHARKS

Hundreds of millions of years ago, Earth was much different from now. The continents were jammed together into one landmass. Later, they began moving apart. The land was covered in simple plants. The warm, shallow seas were teeming with life forms such as sponges and jellyfish.

About 550 MYA, the first fish evolved. They had flexible backbones and fins for swimming. They developed **gills** to breathe underwater. The first fish didn't have jaws. They looked very different from modern fish and sharks.

Conodonts were jawless fish that lived sometime between about 500 and 443 MYA.

ACANTHODIANS

These early fish continued to evolve. By 450 MYA, the oceans were filled with different types of bony fish. The first fish with jaws developed. They are known as acanthodians.

Acanthodians weren't shaped like the sharks of today. But they did have sharklike jaws and rows of sharp teeth. Their skin was covered by toothlike spines. They had skeletons made of **cartilage**. All modern sharks have skeletons of cartilage, not bone. Acanthodians weren't actually sharks.

Scientists have found acanthodian fossils of spines, scales, and teeth. This drawing is a guess at what the fish really looked like.

But all sharks living today evolved from this

early fish.

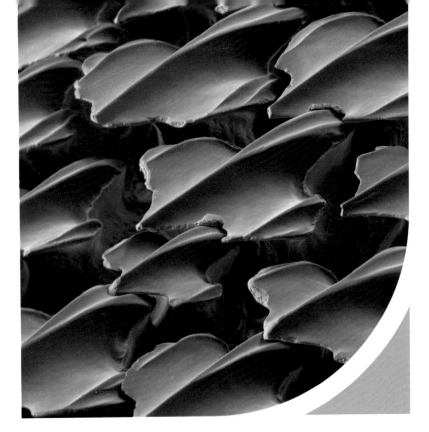

A microscopic view of the scales on a modern spiny dogfish shark

EARLY SHARKS

Paleontologists don't know what the earliest known shark looked like. They only have a few fossilized shark scales from 420 MYA. These scales have been found in Siberia and Mongolia. Shark scales, including these fossils, are shaped a bit like teeth. That's one way scientists know the scales came from early sharks.

Experts know a little more about *Leonodus*. They have found fossil teeth from this early shark in Europe. The two-pronged teeth date to 400 MYA. Scientists think this shark may have been shaped like an eel

FOSSIL RECORD

Fossils are the remains or traces of plants and animals that lived long ago. Experts have found fossils of shark teeth, scales, and skeletons. Because cartilage is softer than bone, it breaks down faster. That means scientists find fewer fossils of body parts made of cartilage, such as shark skeletons.

and lived in fresh water. Many of the earliest sharks were shaped like eels.

Over time, sharks began to look more familiar. Their teeth, gills, and skin became more like the sharks of today. Marine biologist David Shiffman says, "The fossil record tells us that by 370 million years ago ancient sharks would have been recognizably related to the sharks we know today."[1]

More than 350 MYA, a new type of shark emerged. *Cladoselache* looked a bit like modern sharks. A fossil hunter found a well-preserved fossil of this fish in the 1880s

An illustration of what Cladoselache *probably looked like*

in Ohio. The fossil included skeleton parts, skin, and even muscles.

From fossils, paleontologists know that *Cladoselache* was shaped like a torpedo, not an eel. It was about 5 feet (1.5 m) long. It had triangular fins on its body and a strong tail fin. It had large eyes, a short snout, and lots of teeth. It had at least five gills, and some fossils show seven.

It was probably a strong swimmer that hunted by sight. It likely preyed on small fish. *Cladoselache* swam the oceans until it went extinct about 250 MYA.

SHARK EVOLUTION

Ancient shark **species** lived in both fresh and salt water. They evolved and changed over millions of years. Many shark species appeared and disappeared. Occasionally, the environment on Earth changed drastically. When that happened, many plants and animals died, including sharks. "**Extinctions** that obliterated wide swaths of life have reshaped Earth's history," writes journalist Katherine Kornei.[2] Some shark species survived these mass extinctions. The survivors continued to evolve.

DRAGON TONGUES

Most shark fossils are teeth. That's because teeth are hard and because sharks have many of them. They grow new teeth all their lives. The old teeth fall out. A shark can have as many as 40,000 teeth during its life. Long ago, people thought fossilized shark teeth were the hardened tongues of dragons.

2

THE AGE OF
SHARKS

The Carboniferous Period began about 359 MYA. Prehistoric sharks dominated the oceans. Over time, many unique species developed. By the end of this period, 299 MYA, about 45 types of sharks had emerged. This time is often called the golden age of sharks.

Most early sharks had been shaped like eels or torpedoes. But during the golden age, sharks evolved into lots of strange shapes. Some of the weirdest sharks that ever lived existed during these years.

Stethacanthus fossils have been found in North America, Asia, and Europe. This creature lived during the golden age of sharks.

GOLDEN AGE

One of the strangest sharks of this time was *Stethacanthus*. It lived about 350 MYA. This odd-looking shark was about 3 feet (1 m) long. It had a spiky, flat fin on top of its head that looked kind of like a toothbrush. The fin's flat surface was covered with tiny scales like hooks. *Stethacanthus* also had a patch of these scales on its forehead. Long, streamer-like body parts trailed from the shark's side fins.

Experts don't know exactly what the strange top fin was used for. Some think it may have been used as a weapon.

Or the hooklike scales could have acted as suckers. Perhaps the shark used its fin to attach to larger sharks or fish to catch a ride. Or maybe the shark used the fin to attract a mate.

Falcatus, another ancient creature, lived around 325 MYA. The male of this species grew a long, sharp horn from its upper

SHARKS AND OTHER FISH

Most fish have skeletons made of bone. All sharks, however, have skeletons made of cartilage. Cartilage is lighter than bone. That helps sharks float and swim long distances. Most fish have one gill slit on each side of their bodies. Sharks have five or more slits on each side.

back. The horn curved forward over the top of the shark's head. Experts think the shark used this horn when finding a mate.

One ancient shark is nicknamed nature's buzz saw. *Helicoprion* had a spiraling mouth of jagged teeth. It lived from about 290 to 270 MYA. Paleontologists have studied the shark's teeth fossils. They think that when *Helicoprion* closed its jaws, the rows of long teeth rotated like a buzz saw.

Edestid was another strange prehistoric shark. This one lived from about 313 to 307 MYA. Its single row of sharp teeth grew in long, curved jaws. The top jaw curved

An artist's idea of the prehistoric shark Helicoprion

up, and the bottom jaw curved down.

When its jaws closed, the teeth may have

fitted together like the pinking shears used

in sewing.

Edestid was part of the genus Edestus. For years, scientists have debated how Edestus sharks chewed their food. No other known creature has a jaw quite like this one.

"Taken together, all these 'saws, scissors and sharks' would seem to suggest that [sharks] of more than 250 million years ago were far stranger than anything alive today," says science writer Riley Black.[3]

A mass extinction ended the golden age of sharks about 250 MYA. It was one of the biggest extinction events in Earth's history. About 95 percent of all living things were wiped out. That included many of these odd shark species. Only a few shark species survived. But as their ocean habitat changed, those remaining sharks began to adapt to new environments. They continued to evolve to look more like the sharks

of today.

MODERN TRAITS

After the extinction event of 250 MYA,

mammals and birds began to appear.

Dinosaurs thundered across the land. Huge

marine reptiles shared the seas with fish

and sharks. A dozen new species of sharks

appeared during the Jurassic Period, from

201 to 145 MYA. These sharks began to

resemble the large, fast-moving sharks that

dominate the seas today.

The hybodus fraasi shark was part of the hybodont family. It probably weighed between 100 and 200 pounds (45 to 91 kg).

The sharks that survived the extinction event moved into new oceans and fresh water around the world. As they adapted, they began to evolve many traits of today's modern sharks. The earliest sharks had rigid jaws. These new sharks developed more flexible jaws that could open wider. That meant they could attack and eat bigger prey. Bigger sharks evolved to feed on huge reptiles and whales.

Many sharks of this period became fast swimmers. They developed strong tail fins. Their mouths moved under their snouts for a more streamlined bullet shape.

The most common group of sharks during the Jurassic were the hybodonts. The largest hybodont species grew to 6 feet (2 m) long. Hybodonts had a row of sharp teeth that are typical of many sharks. They also had teeth that were flat and stout. Their name comes from Greek words meaning *humped tooth*.

SHARKS AND RAYS

Sharks and rays are related. Both evolved from the shark group known as hybodonts. During the Jurassic, they began to evolve into separate species. Rays look like flat sharks. Many are shaped like kites. Skates and sawfish are also related to sharks.

3

MONSTERS OF THE SEAS

The Cretaceous Period followed the Jurassic. It lasted from 145 to 65 MYA. Sharks during this time were diverse. They lived in salt water and fresh water. Some fast sharks hunted other fish, sharks, and whales. Others moved slowly along the bottom of the ocean. They ate small

sea animals.

Some strange sharks appeared and

disappeared during this time. One is

known as the Ginsu shark. It lived from

The scientific name for the Ginsu shark is Cretoxyrhina mantelli.

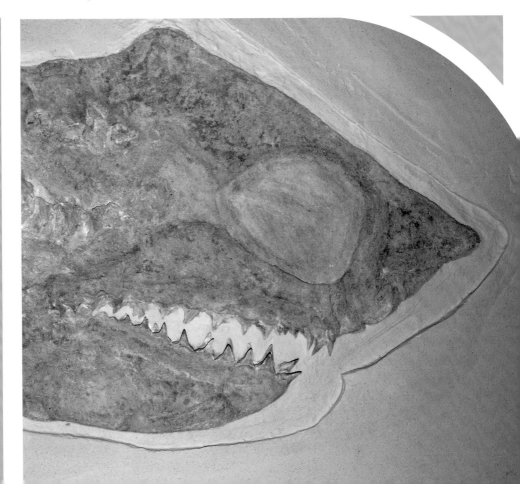

about 107 to 73 MYA. Scientists know a lot about this extinct shark from a nearly complete fossil spine and 250 teeth. Ginsu sharks were about 20 feet (6 m) long and fearsome. They had knife-sharp, 2-inch (5-cm) curved teeth. Their teeth sliced and diced large prey, much like the brand of kitchen knife they were named after.

In 2021, paleontologists discovered a prehistoric shark with fins that looked like wings. This species from the Cretaceous Period appeared to be part shark, part manta ray. It had a strong, sharklike tail, but the shark was wider than it was long.

A prehistoric shark discovered in 2021 had fins that looked like those of a modern manta ray, shown here.

Its winglike fins spread out from its sides,

like the fins on modern manta rays.

RISE OF MODERN SHARKS

Modern-looking sharks appeared during
the Cretaceous Period, too. That included
a new family of sharks known as lamnids.
Lamnids were strong, swift predators. They
had large bodies with powerful fins and
pointed heads. On the sides of their heads
were large gill slits. Under their heads were
large mouths with rows of sharp teeth.
Lamnids looked like modern sharks. They
are the ancestors of today's mako sharks,
bull sharks, and great white sharks.

Another mass extinction took place
at the end of the Cretaceous. Dinosaurs

The modern salmon shark descended from lamnids.

died off. Many shark species went extinct.

But others lived on, including the lamnids.

Then, about 20 MYA, a new shark

appeared. Megalodon was the largest and

most terrifying predator the oceans had

ever seen.

MEGALODON

Megalodon is the most famous prehistoric shark. Its name means *big tooth*, and it ruled the oceans for millions of years. Megalodon was the largest shark or fish that has ever existed.

This huge ancient shark looked like a great white shark but was bigger than a whale. It probably grew 50 to 60 feet (15 to 18 m) long and weighed more than 66,000 pounds (30,000 kg). It also had an enormous mouth, explained Hans Sues, a paleobiologist at the Smithsonian National Museum of Natural History. Sues said,

This museum exhibit shows how big megalodon's jaw really was.

"A megalodon mouth is so big that you could swim into it without touching any of the teeth. It literally could swallow a small car without having to chomp down on it."[4]

Experts study fossil teeth to learn about megalodon. The shark's teeth were sharp and triangular. They looked like the teeth of modern great white sharks. So scientists think megalodon was similar to great whites in some ways. At 7 inches (18 cm) long, though, its teeth were three times larger than a great white's teeth. A shark with teeth that big would have to be at least three times larger than a great white, which is about 18 feet (5.5 m) long.

BITE FORCE

Megalodon didn't just have huge, sharp teeth. It had a big bite, too. It could open its mouth 9 feet (2.7 m) wide. It could chomp down with more force than any other creature that has ever lived.

A modern great white shark shows its sharp teeth.

Megalodon looked like the great white.

But it is probably more closely related to

modern mako sharks.

Megalodon was big enough to hunt the

largest animals in the sea, including whales.

This shark's huge jaws were lined with rows

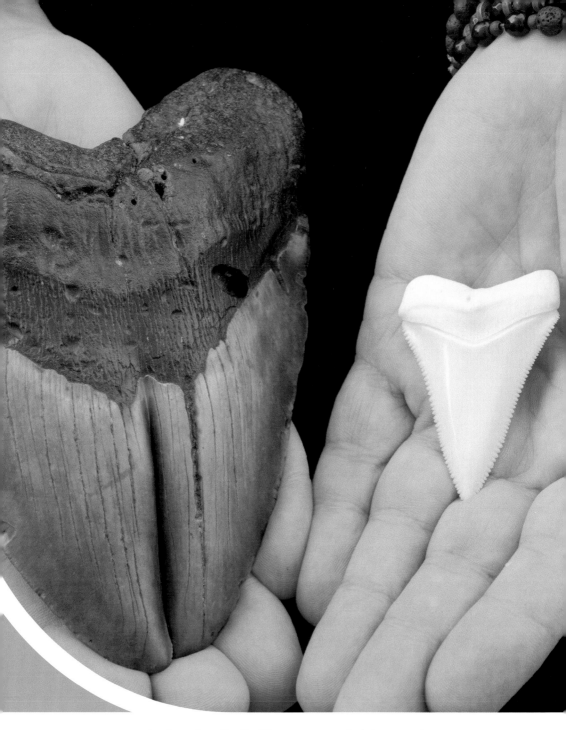

A megalodon tooth (left) was much bigger than a great white shark's tooth.

of hundreds of sharp teeth—perfect for slicing chunks of flesh from prey.

Scientists think megalodon had died off by two MYA. Earth's climate changed, and sea levels changed. Coastal waters, where young megalodons lived, became more shallow. Megalodon may have not been able to adapt to the changing habitat.

SURVIVING EXTINCTIONS

Megalodon went extinct, but sharks as a group lived on. The key to their success was diversity. They lived in different types and depths of water. Sharks ate lots of different foods, from whales to tiny plankton. This diversity meant some sharks could survive big changes to the oceans.

4

LIVING FOSSILS

Sharks have survived five great extinctions that killed many other species. According to marine biologist David Shiffman, "After each mass extinction, many shark species died, but the ones that survived went on to live and evolve further until the next mass extinction."[5]

Today, more than 500 species of sharks

live on Earth. Some are as small as a

human hand. Whale sharks grow to 39 feet

(12 m) long. Some sharks even live under

the Arctic ice. Most sharks have evolved

Pygmy sharks are some of the smallest sharks in the world. The pygmy shark on top is an adult female. The bottom one is a baby.

PREHISTORIC ERAS AND PERIODS

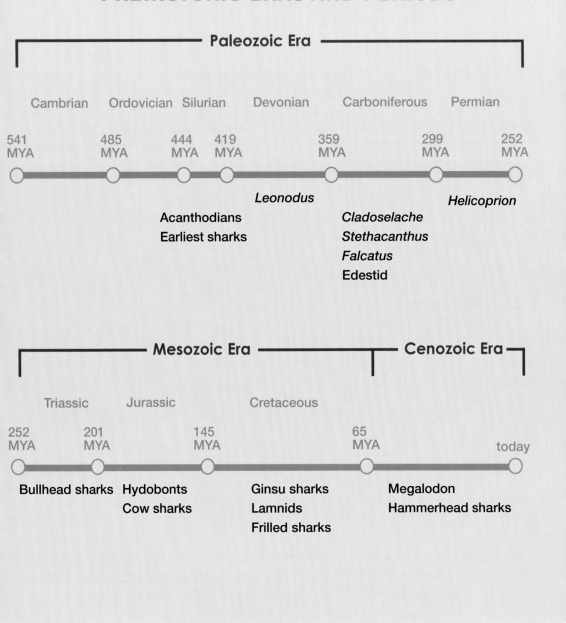

In history, an era is a long period of time with some consistent feature. The Mesozoic Era, for example, is sometimes called the Age of Reptiles.

to have long bodies, strong fins, and sharp teeth. But some sharks have changed very little from their prehistoric relatives. They look like living fossils.

COW SHARKS

One example of a living fossil is the cow shark. Cow sharks appeared during the Jurassic Period and have changed very little since then. Most modern sharks have five pairs of gill slits. Present-day cow sharks have six or seven pairs, just like their primitive ancestors.

The broadnose sevengill cow shark has ancestors from 300 MYA. It lives in warm, shallow waters.

The sixgill shark is the largest type of cow shark. It has a blunt head and a powerful body, with one top fin and a small bottom fin near its tail. These sharks are about 16 feet (4.9 m) long. The sixgill shark is light brown or gray with bright blue-green eyes. It lives in deep waters.

The sixgill has six comb-shaped rows of pointy teeth. It uses its sawlike teeth to catch and eat fish, smaller sharks, squid, and shellfish. It can even prey on seals.

FRILLED SHARKS

Frilled sharks today look similar to their ancestors from more than 350 MYA. The frilled shark has a long, eellike shape, like

NEWEST FAMILY MEMBERS

Hammerhead sharks are the most recent addition to the shark family. They first appeared around 20 MYA. They are also among the strangest-looking sharks. Their wide-set eyes allow them to see better than other sharks.

A drawing of a frilled shark

the earliest prehistoric sharks. It grows to about 6 feet (1.8 m) long. It has one top fin far back on its body and one fin underneath. Its snout is blunt. The shark's mouth is at the front of its head, and its nostrils are on top. Today's sharks usually have mouths and nostrils on the bottom of their heads.

Most modern sharks have sharp teeth shaped like triangles. Frilled sharks have the strange teeth of their prehistoric relatives. Each tooth has three long points. These teeth are perfect for grabbing squid and fish as they swim past. Then the shark can swallow them whole.

The frilled shark lives in deep, dark waters. It has six pairs of long, frilly gills. That's how this ancient-looking shark got its name.

BULLHEAD SHARKS

The bullhead family of sharks first appeared about 220 MYA. This is around the same time when the first dinosaurs appeared. Bullhead sharks today look much like their ancestors, the hybodonts of the Jurassic Period.

One species of bullhead shark is the Port Jackson shark. It has a blunt snout that looks a bit like a pig's nose. Its head is large and bulky compared to its narrowing body. Dark patches run across its eyes and down the shark's sides. The markings make the shark look as if it is wearing a harness.

The Port Jackson shark has two types of teeth. In the front of its jaw are small, pointed teeth. In the back, the teeth are broad and flat. This shark can grab prey with its sharp front teeth and crush it with the back teeth. Port Jackson sharks live off the southern coast of Australia. They cruise the bottom of the ocean, where they

SPEEDY SWIMMERS

The shark is one of the ocean's fastest creatures. Most sharks are shaped like slim torpedoes with a strong tail at the end. Their cartilage skeletons are light. Their entire bodies are covered in smooth scales. These adaptations allow sharks to speed through the water.

Port Jackson sharks rest on the ocean floor near Australia.

feed on sea urchins, starfish, and other creatures. One of the most unusual things about this shark is that it can eat and breathe at the same time. Most sharks can't do that.

These living fossils provide a glimpse into the past, when strange-looking sharks swam and hunted in the planet's ancient waters. As scientists study these animals and fossils from long ago, they learn more about Earth's history and about prehistoric creatures. The more we learn about prehistoric sharks, the more we will know about sharks living today.

GLOSSARY

cartilage
strong, elastic tissue

evolved
changed slowly and naturally over a very long time

extinction
the dying out or coming to an end of a species of plants, animals, or insects

gills
pairs of organs next to a fish or shark's mouth through which it breathes

MYA
million years ago

paleontologists
scientists who study fossils

predator
an animal that hunts other animals for food

species
a group of animals or plants that are similar and can mate and have offspring

SOURCE NOTES

CHAPTER ONE: THE FIRST SHARKS

1. David Shiffman, "Sharks," *Smithsonian Ocean*, n.d. https://ocean.si.edu.

2. Katherine Kornei, "Sharks Almost Went the Way of the Dinosaurs 19 Million Years Ago," *New York Times*, June 3, 2021. www.nytimes.com.

CHAPTER TWO: THE AGE OF SHARKS

3. Riley Black, "These Prehistoric Sharks Had Jaws Shaped Like Circular Saws and Sawtoothed Scissors," *Smithsonian Magazine*, April 2, 2021. www.smithsonianmag.com.

CHAPTER THREE: MONSTERS OF THE SEAS

4. Quoted in Frankie Schembri, "Could the Star of the Meg Really Bite a Ship in Half? We Took a Paleobiologist to the New Movie to Find Out," *Science*, August 9, 2018. www.science.org.

CHAPTER FOUR: LIVING FOSSILS

5. Shiffman, "Sharks."

FOR FURTHER RESEARCH

BOOKS

Tammy Gagne, *Megalodon and Other Prehistoric Sharks*. North Mankato, MN: Capstone Press, 2022.

Yang Yang and Zhao Chung, *The Secrets of Ancient Sea Monsters: PNSO Encyclopedia for Children*. New York: Brown Books Kids, 2021.

Kathleen Weidner Zoehfeld, *Prehistoric: Dinosaurs, Megalodons, and Other Fascinating Creatures of the Deep Past*. Greenbelt, MD: What on Earth Books, 2019.

INTERNET SOURCES

Riley Black, "These Prehistoric Sharks Had Jaws Shaped Like Circular Saws and Sawtoothed Scissors," *Smithsonian Magazine*, April 2, 2021. www.smithsonianmag.com.

Devon Bowen, "Evolution's Ultimate Predator: Here Are Our Top 10 Prehistoric Sharks," *Two Oceans Aquarium*, October 14, 2020. www.aquarium.co.za.

Josh Davis, "Megalodon: The Truth About the Largest Shark That Ever Lived," *Natural History Museum London*, n.d. www.nhm.ac.uk.

WEBSITES

Natural History Museum, London

www.nhm.ac.uk/discover/shark-evolution-a-450-million-year
-timeline.html

The Natural History Museum's website includes research about Earth's geology and life, including a timeline of shark evolution.

Shark Research Institute

www.sharks.org

The Shark Research Institute is a shark conservation nonprofit that focuses on scientific research. The site includes news and information about research, education, conservation, and legislation.

Smithsonian Ocean: "Sharks"

https://ocean.si.edu/ocean-life/sharks-rays/sharks

The Ocean Portal is part of the Smithsonian Institution's Ocean Initiative and focuses on everything about the ocean. The section on sharks includes information on shark anatomy, diversity, and evolution.

INDEX

IMAGE CREDITS

Cover: © Richard Bizley/Science Source

5: © Warpaint/Shutterstock Images

7: © Elenarts/Shutterstock Images

8: © Connah/iStockphoto

11: © W. Scott McGill/Shutterstock Images

13: © Lilya Butenko/Shutterstock Images

15: © Serafima Antipova/Shutterstock Images

16: © Eye of Science/Science Source

19: © Jaime Chirinos/Science Source

23: © James Keuther/Science Source

27: © James Keuther/Science Source

28: © Michael Rosskothen/Shutterstock Images

31: © Jaime Chirinos/Science Source

35: © Tom Stack/Alamy

37: © Dive Pic/iStockphoto

39: © Warren Metcalf/Shutterstock Images

41: © Mulevich/Shutterstock Images

43: © MG SG/Shutterstock Images

44: © Mark Kostich/iStockphoto

47: © Doug Perrine/Blue Planet Archive

48: © Red Line Editorial

50: © Greg Amptman/Shutterstock Images

52: © 3D Sam 79/Shutterstock Images

56: © Nigel Marsh/iStockphoto

ABOUT THE AUTHOR

Yvette LaPierre lives in North Dakota with her family. Her day job is academic advisor for the Indians Into Medicine program at the University of North Dakota School of Medicine and Health Sciences. She is the author of more than twenty nonfiction books for young readers.